TRIUMPH TRIPLES

TRIUMPH TRIPLES

Andrew Morland & Peter Henshaw

OSPREY
AUTOMOTIVE

First published in Great Britain in 1995
by Osprey, an imprint of Reed Consumer
Books Limited, Michelin House,
81 Fulham Road, London SW3 6RB and
Auckland, Melbourne, Singapore and Toronto.

ISBN 1 85532 428 8

Photographs by Andrew Morland
Text by Peter Henshaw
Project editor Shaun Barrington
Editors Simon McAuslane and Julia North
Page design Paul Kime/Ward Peacock
Partnership

Printed in Hong Kong

ACKNOWLEDGEMENTS

Thanks go to many triple owners for allowing us to photograph their bikes;
Richard Cant, Neil Payne, Neil Townsend, Brian Gilling, Pete Cornock, Tony
Pettit and Les Williams. Also to Tim Smithells at Sussex Triples, Trevor
Gleadhall of L.P. Williams and Titch Masters of Somerset Forge Ltd. Without
them, the book would not have been possible. Special thanks go to Andy Hayman
of Riders of Bridgewater, for lending us the latest Triumph triples to photograph,
to Bruno Tagliaferri of Triumph for all his help.

Andrew Morland & Peter Henshaw, September 1994

Pictures on pages 99-100 by Phil Masters. With thanks to Alan Cathcart for
additional information.

Half title page
*Hinckley put a lot of effort into quality,
especially the paint (it was all brought
in-house in 1994), and it paid off*

Title page
*A choice of Trident 750, 850 or 1,000cc
Hyde engine finishes off the Harrier,
which costs about £10,000 complete.
(See page 79)*

Right
*1970 Trident with the Bonnie tank. The
downpipes were unchanged, but the ray
gun silencers were ditched in favour of
old-style ones. Despite the appearance
these were actually unique to the
triples. (See page 25)*

For a catalogue of all books published by Osprey Automotive
please write to:

**The Marketing Department, Reed Consumer Books,
1st Floor, Michelin House, 81 Fulham Road, London SW3 6RB**

Introduction

Triumph is becoming indelibly associated with three-cylinder motorcycles. It wasn't always like that – even when Tridents were still rolling out of Meriden, the old Triumph was seen as a maker of twins, for which the triple was an addendum, and not a replacement. The difference now is that three-cylinder bikes are at the heart of the range, accounting for roughly 85-90 % of sales.

By contrast, the old Trident was never a huge seller; its reputation extended beyond its numbers and, right to the end, was always outsold by the twins. There were even those who refused to see it (especially the early slab-sided T150) as a real Triumph.

Nevertheless, it's tempting to imagine a sort of Triumph triple inheritance, floating across the ether between Meriden and Hinckley (they are, after all, only ten miles apart). Unfortunately it's nonsense. There are similarities apart from the name on the tank (notably the throaty howl they both make), but these are there more by accident than design, and far outweighed by the many differences between the two.

The engines share nothing, apart from the number of cylinders. The old one used pushrods; its successor has twin overhead cams and also sports a balance shaft. In engineering terms, they are a generation apart. The new design team was completely different (said to come from disparate engineering backgrounds), and only one or two ex-Meriden personnel found a job at Hinckley. The new team started with a clean sheet, whereas the Meriden men were forced to base their triple on twin parts. Then there's the market – the first Trident created an impact because it was bigger, heavier and faster than just about anything else (this is before the CB750 arrived). Yet the current model is no more intimidating than countless others. In 750 Trident terms, the old bike was an expensive flagship, but the new one is the cheapest in the range. The companies are different too. In management jargon, the new Triumph is 'market-led' – looking for niches, and filling them quickly, with an emphasis on quality and reliablity, with a view to what people actually want to buy. It is also a relatively young company, with only a few older members of staff. So do new and old Triumph triples have anything in common at all?

Well, both were based on the modular concept. The old one started off with the same 63x80mm bore x stroke as the Speed Twin, and the 67x70 it eventually adopted was tentatively planned as the basis of a 250 single and 500 twin. Bert Hopwood's plan for an all-new BSA/Triumph range for the seventies was also modular. Also, the addition of a cylinder to the current Triumph triples produces the four pot version. Both, too, used existing technology, with no great innovations; the T150 owed a great deal to pushrod twins, sharing their drum brakes and Lucas electrics. Meanwhile, the Hinckley bikes' four valve per cylinder, DOHC layout has been part of big Japanese bikes for many years. Meriden used existing parts because it was the quickest way of bringing out a CB750 competitor; and Hinckley did likewise, for their use guaranteed reliability and thus helped to establish a good reputation quickly.

There is one other similarity between the old and new Triumph triples. One hesitates to use the old 'character' cliché, but it's true that all of these machines are great fun to ride, offering an experience quite different to that of the Japanese, European and American alternatives. They're revvy, but with decent mid-range power; not vibratory like a big twin, but with just enough of a raw edge to remind you that you're sitting behind a big four-stroke. Best of all, the three-cylinder howl of a Trident is again back on the road.

Right

The most famous Triumph triple of all. Slippery Sam started life in 1970 as a Production Racer, and eventually went on to win five TTs

Contents

Prototypes & T150

Many people regarded the Trident as being Triumph's 'last gasp', rushed into production to meet encroaching Japanese competition. In fact, it was anything but; prototype engines were running nearly four years before the triples finally went on sale. A misguided, sidetracked management conspired to keep it first in a corner of the Experimental Department, then under Umberslade Hall's somewhat unproductive stylists.

First Thoughts

It was the fruitful partnership of Hele and Hopwood which made the triple become a reality. Doug Hele was a brilliant development engineer, a lateral thinker with long motorcycle experience. Under Bert Hopwood (then General Manager at Meriden) he was given the scope to exercise his talents. Hopwood too was an engineer, so he understood Hele's thinking, but also had the seniority to push good ideas at board level. The two instituted a last golden era at Triumph, producing what many feel to be the ultimate development of the Triumph twin (or indeed any British twin) by the end of the sixties.

Neither man was blind to competition, especially from Japan, which was why, in late 1963, they suggested a 750cc triple, developed directly from the existing bikes. Managing Director Edward Turner was not impressed; this is perhaps not surprising, as he was the man who had acted as Godfather to the twins, seeing them through tremendous pre- and post-war success. But he was also the man who had recently visited Honda in Japan, and had a very clear idea of the coming threat. For whatever reason, he turned down the triple, and it wasn't until the following year, when Turner had retired and been replaced by Harry Sturgeon, that the triple got its chance.

Bert Hopwood later recalled how a meeting of senior managers was brought to a grinding halt when someone casually let drop that Honda was working on a 750-4. Sturgeon wasn't a motorcycle man, but he was a good manager, and immediately gave the go-ahead for prototype triples to be built up. Doug Hele and a small development team got to work straightaway, and within a year the first engine was running.

Jeff Jones on his 748cc BSA Rocket 3, flying though the air over Ballaugh Bridge in the TT Formula 1 race in the Isle of Man – 2 June, 1979

First Prototypes

The first prototype, named P1, produced an impressive 58bhp at 7,250rpm; particularly impressive, as it retained the original pre-unit 500's long 80mm stroke dimensions, plus its narrow 63mm bore, and a cast-iron cylinder barrel. It was true, as Norman Hyde later recalled, that the 63x80 set-up made for a narrower engine, but there was more to it than that. Maximising commonality with the twins was the quickest way of building the triple, and it was this modular idea which was central to the Hele/Hopwood approach.

It was also the reason they took the apparently radical three-cylinder route in the first place. They needed more power, but knew that expanding the existing twins to 750s would be asking too much of an ageing design. An all-new engine, on the other hand, would take years to reach the market, but a three-cylinder version of the twin would take comparatively little time to make into metal. Once on sale, this stop-gap would allow time for the design of a fully modern machine. There were other good reasons for three-cylinders – usefully narrower than an across-the-frame four, and far smoother than the twins.

Width seems to have been one of the design team's preoccupations (understandable after a diet of simple, narrow twins) and one of Doug Hele's first acts was to design a very compact clutch, to reduce width at the footrest position. Sensibly, in view of the power, it was a car-type diaphragm single plate unit, in place of the traditional wet multi-plater. There was also a car-type distributor (another carry-over from the pre-unit 500) and gear primary drive. In this form, with less than 1,000 miles under its wheels, the prototype was shown at a Metropolitan Police day at MIRA. Unfortunately, its very noisy clutch and primary drive was enough to put off some police buyers – maybe waiting a year for the preview would have been wiser.

As with any prototype, there were problems. The primary drive noise was caused by the heat expansion of aluminium Crank and gearbox shafts moved apart by 0.020in-0.025in, making the gears sound "like two dustbin lids being banged together!", according to Norman Hyde, who was part of Hele's team. Changing to a triplex chain primary drive proved to be the solution. Meanwhile, a new aluminium cylinder barrel saved weight and put an end to head gasket failures, the problem being the different expansion rates of the aluminium head and iron barrel. The distributor gave way to three sets of points mounted on the timing end of the exhaust cam (just like the latest twins, in other words) – the points cover even had three Phillips screws where the twins had two!

Mr Alistair Frame on the Bee Bee Racing 830cc BSA Rocket 3 at Creg-Ny-Baa in the rain. The TT World Championship Formula 1 race – 31 May, 1980

To improve breathing, the bore/stroke dimensions were changed to 67x70mm. The design team hoped to use these as the basis of a modular family (250 single, 500 twin, 750 triple) all sharing components to keep costs down, and all keeping the BSA/Triumph marque afloat until more modern successors were ready. In order to take full advantage of the bigger bore, inlet ports and carburettors were enlarged.

Soon the prototype was almost ready for production, but its development was delayed by other projects, only some of which were worth pursuing. With Harry Sturgeon seriously ill and out of action, Chairman Eric Turner decreed that work be done on boring out the twins to 750 and giving them ohc valvegear.

This came to nothing. There was also the other triple, Doug Hele's ohc 250 designed for 14,000rpm, a six-speed gearbox and electric start. (In the event, Eric Turner killed it in favour of a hotted up BSA C15.) BSA/Triumph US importers, meanwhile, were pushing hard for a group entry for the Daytona races. All of this took up valuable time, which could have been used to put the triple into production, and which Honda was using to finalise its own 750.

When the final go-ahead was given, however, the triple was sent for restyling. This meant a lengthy sojourn at Umberslade Hall. Umberslade (or 'Slumberglade' as some knew it) with its 300 staff and £1 million annual running costs, has come to symbolise everything that was wrong with BSA/Triumph in the late sixties. Overstaffed, and well away from

Above

Triples are still racing at Daytona in the classic events. This competitor and his ex-works Rob North-framed bike are ready for scrutineering in 1994

Left

Well preserved and race ready, twenty years on. This picture could have been taken in 1974, but for the Goodridge hoses

Above right

Restored T150 in 1969 trim, outside the oft-photographed Kenilworth Castle. The only non-standard parts are the handlebars – original bikes had US-style high risers, which were trendy but didn't do much for high speed handling

Right

Aquamarine was the name of that first Trident colour. This particular bike was restored by Trevor Gleadhall, current owner of triple specialists L.P. Williams

the realities at Meriden and Small Heath, its committees decided the triple needed a complete re-style. Consultants Ogle Design were brought in. It was a company not without talent (having penned the milestone Scimitar GTE), but with no motorcycle experience, and the result was a slab-sided, squared-off, heavy-looking bike.

The 'bread bin' tank seemed to emphasise the bike's weight and width, and there had been a fairly obvious attempt to distance this latest BSA/Triumph from the twins. In doing so, the stylists failed to realise that the spare, balanced look was a major reason why people bought the old bikes, and Triumphs in particular. This became clear once the triple was on sale and, within a couple of years, the Americans got the traditionally styled Trident they wanted, although UK customers had to wait for the T160.

Launch at Last

In the mid-nineties, with 58bhp being less than half the output of a good sports 750, it's easy to forget the Trident's impact when it was launched in September 1968. Testers wrote breathlessly of 80mph in second, 110 in third, and having to hang on desperately to the handlebars as this "big, fast groundshaker of a machine" (*Cycle World*) leapt forward. Compared to the twins (as, inevitably, it was) the Trident came over as incredibly fast, very smooth and revvy. Heavy, too, but everyone agreed that, once under way, this was hardly noticeable and that the new bike handled well. Its springing might be a little soft *in extremis* (especially two-up) and

15

Left

The big side cover was a styling feature, suspiciously similar to Hondas of the same age. But underneath, the air filter still carried the same old chrome embellishment, just like the twins. The French horn is not an original feature

Above

The beautiful 8-inch twin leading shoe front drum came straight from the twins. It was the standard T150 fitment for three years, until the troubled company was able to fit a disc

ground clearance was limited – its centre stand and silencers touched down too early, but overall it came out with good marks.

It was a particularly good showing when one considers the opposition. As a result of corporate indecision, the Trident was not the first superbike. The Commando had been on sale months previously (and a full year before the British could buy a triple), while Honda's four, with its extra cylinder, disc brake and electric start, appeared at almost the same time as the new BSA/Triumph. Both were substantially cheaper and just as powerful, while the Honda was (inevitably) less prone to temperament. On the other hand, it was a brave CB rider who tried to stay with a triple on twisty roads, while the Norton's long-stroke twin just didn't have the same high speed stamina. Some said that the Commando was quicker up to about 90mph, thanks to its superior low/mid range torque; ultimately, however, the triple would rev higher and run faster.

All three bikes were precursors of a new breed of motorcycle, with new levels of performance and sophistication. Within a few years, the other three Japanese makers had joined in (as well as big Ducatis and Laverdas) all of which served to make the triples look prematurely middle-aged. Even before this later onslaught, early sales were disappointing. Many people have blamed the styling (the Americans in particular took exception to it), but there was also the high price and very limited early production – at first, just fifty engines were being built a week. This was partly because they were extremely complex and difficult to make (as Doug Hele was to point out, the designers were hampered by ageing

Right

150mph speedometer and 10,000rpm rev counter had more relevance to the Trident than other Triumphs, but were still a bit optimistic – ammeter and steering damper are traditional Triumph fitments

Above

A substantial grabrail was a very necessary part if you carried a passenger and used all of the Trident's prodigious acceleration

production methods and tools), and partly because of the need to build two distinct versions (see below). Then there was the specification – no electric start or disc brake. The engine was indeed wonderful, but sharing things like brakes and forks with the old bikes marked the triples out as stop-gaps. None of this would have mattered with a 1966 launch, (which could have been possible) but things had moved on.

Rocket III

It was the Americans who insisted on a distinct BSA variant of the triple. This was understandable, given that the BSA/Triumph dealers in the States were independent and in most cases wished to remain so. Unfortunately, it seemed that a different tank and a change of badging was not enough. Incredibly, the Rocket III had a different frame to the Trident (duplex, not single, downtubes); the cylinder barrel was tilted forward (which meant different crankcase castings); the timing side engine/gearbox covers were different too, with each needing their own castings. It was all very expensive and time-consuming. It is alleged that much time was wasted simply switching from production of one engine to another. These difficulties dashed Bert Hopwood's hopes for a modular range. Despite all the effort and expense, only 7,000 Rocket IIIs were sold as opposed to 45,000 T150 Tridents. One internal company report, blames this on lack of components, however, rather than failure in the market. Nevertheless, manufacture of the the fastest production BSA ever ceased in 1972.

Rescue Attempts: Racers, Restyles & T150V

Troubled though it may have been (losses and redundancies were signalling the beginning of the end of the BSA Group), BSA/Triumph wasn't completely blind to the triple's failings. Within a couple of years, some of these had been addressed. US-bound bikes got more traditional twin-type styling (and dealers offered tank/side panel/silencer kits to existing owners), a five-speed gearbox appeared, and triples went racing.

The last move was a smart one, given Triumph's earlier success with the 500 twin at Daytona, though in usual Group fashion, Doug Hele's Experimental Dept was given just three months to prepare for a full-scale onslaught on the American 1970 season. It was an expensive (that first season cost $1 million) but successful route. For a short time, triples dominated big capacity racing in both Europe and the US. Over the next couple of years, they were to score wins in classics like the Daytona, Bol d'Or and Production TT. Also in that first year, BSA/Triumph took the first five places in the American racing championship.

The racers themselves had a curious mix of both factory and privateer know-how. Rob North built the frames, Quaife advised on the five-speed gear cluster, while Hele's team at Meriden worked wonders with the engine. The North frames (reportedly 36 were built for the works bikes) were very effective; lighter, stiffer and (from 1972) two inches lower than the standard ones. At Meriden, the engines got squish cylinder heads, cleaned up ports and a re-angled plug on the central cylinder. Like the twins, the triple engine responded well to tuning, and the result was 80bhp, in a bike that weighed only 400lb compared to 485lb for the roadster. Incidentally, the works bikes went out in both BSA and Triumph colour schemes, some even switching livery more than once!

In 1971, with 84bhp and double disc brakes, victory came at Daytona, (a 1-2-3 that year) the Bol d'Or (thanks to Triumph man Percy Tait) and both Production TT and F750TT races. One measure of the triple's racing success at the time was that every single rider rode one in 1971's Anglo-American Match Race series. But it was a brief blaze of glory; with the company in turmoil, the expensive works team was withdrawn the following year. Bikes were, however, loaned to selected riders, who continued to notch up successes here and there. Who can forget Slippery Sam, the most celebrated bike of all, that won the Production TT an astonishing five times! What the company failed to do was capitalise on the racing successes. There was no race replica triple to cash in on the 1970/71 victories. Sadly, this meant yet another opportunity wasted.

While the triples were doing well on the race tracks, the company that created them was in deep trouble. The waste and mismanagement of the sixties (of which Umberslade Hall was one of the more visible signs) had finally come home to roost. The Meriden men continued development as

Above
Nicely restored detailing on this T150, showing one of the three 27mm Amal Concentrics – choke lever was on the bars

Right
The triples' twin ancestry was clear on this side, though the timing cover did have its distinctive bulge – three sets of cb points lived under the small circular cover

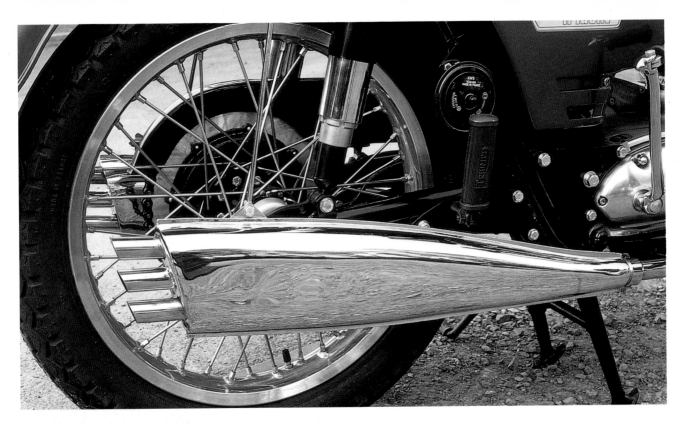

Above left

Those distinctive ray-gun silencers really suited the triple, boosting torque and sounding great. Not everyone liked the look though, "We're sure they could have come up with something better!", said Cycle Guide *in December 1968*

Left

An oil-cooler was always standard, plus alloy barrel to help cooling and keep the weight down

Above

The Rocket Three. This subtly modified 1971 MkII shows the indicators and naked forks of the last BSA triples – a rare bike. Just noticeable here are the tilted forward cylinders of the Rocket (compared to the perpendicular Trident). The reason why the front end of the mudguard looks a little odd is that owner Richard Cant fitted 18-inch wheels – they allow a better choice of modern tyres

best as they could but, to all intents and purposes, the BSA group had collapsed. This meant delays – the five-speed box, for example, was announced as an option in mid-1971, but wasn't actually available until later the following year. It wasn't just fashion that brought in the five-speeder (denoted by the T150V tag) – the triple didn't produce real power until 3,000rpm and the factory had already lowered overall gearing to mask this; more gears allowed closer ratios and a smarter pick-up from low speed. A front disc brake and new colours also marked out the T150V, but the factory also had a more radical derivative on the stocks.

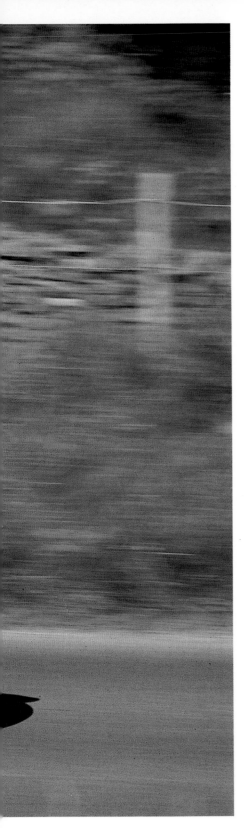

Above

More modifications at the rear end include Marzocchi air-adjustable rear dampers, with the ray gun silencers raised to avoid grounding when leaning hard over

Left

Richard Cant modified his Rocket Three to be ridden, removing the centre stand to give more cornering clearance, fitting Avon Super Venoms (on Akront alloy rims) and a taper roller steering head conversion. A five-speed close ratio gearbox, twin Girling front disc brakes with magnesium calipers. Richard wants to fit rear sets, clip ons and a rear disc brake next year, if finances allow. The suspension changes are there for a reason — this Rocket Three has an 850cc big bore conversion, which the owner reckons gives 120mph. It also returns 28mpg!

Above
*A 1970 Trident, the first reaction to Americans' dislike of the squared-off styling.
Simply using the Bonneville tank and smaller side panels transformed the
appearance – a great improvement*

Left
*Mechanically, the BSA triple was identical to Triumph's, but this one is far from
standard. The shade is Pacific Blue, a Meriden colour*

Above
This particular bike was found rusting away at a dealer in Little Rock, Arkansas. It was brought home and restored by Tim Smithells of Sussex Triples

Right
Although that Bonnie tank is the most obvious change, there were details like chromed mudguard stays and Trident transfers on the side panels

Above
What didn't change was the engine, which looked right from the start. The hard work of Doug Hele and the design team to keep width to a minimum had paid off

Right
Richard Cant's engine looks standard, but inside (as well as the 850 conversion) there are lightened Bonneville pistons, mushroom tappet adjusters and a lightened crank. There's also a belt primary drive and electronic ignition

Above

While the Americans were getting re-styled bikes, everyone else had to make do with the old bread box, albeit with colour scheme changes which improved things a little bit

Right

This is one of the last T150Vs, built at Small Heath under NVT and registered in 1974. A five-speed gearbox was standard now, and about time too

Above

A 10-inch Lockheed front disc was one of the more obvious T150V changes, part of the crash programme of updates made under the new Shawcross regime

Above right

Neat rear end on the T150V, thanks to unobtrusive grabrail and short indicator stanchions. The later type rear light lens is a bit of an eyesore though

Right

Lots of chrome on this T150V and the ungainly Lucas handlebar switches which didn't impress anyone

Above

This particular T150V belongs to Titch Masters, and has covered less than 10,000 miles, hence its completely original appearance

Right

Neil Payne of the Trident and Rocket Three Owners' Club and his 1971 Rocket out on Dartmoor

Above
This was BSA's version of the re-styled US Trident, showing slimmer chromed tank, indicators and megaphone silencers

Left
The light grey frame was BSA's version of the new Umberslade design which was fitted to all big BSA/Triumphs from 1971, with oil kept in the main tube — it handled well but was too tall for many riders

Above

The infamous conical hub drum brakes, part and parcel of the 1971 facelift. Just when BSA/Triumph should have been developing discs, they poured time and money into an all-new drum that was inferior to the old one

Right

The Rocket Three's engine looked the same as a Trident's at a casual glance. But apart from the tilted cylinders, the timing side cover was styled to give a unit construction look — Tridents still had the Triumph stylised gearbox cover

Hurricane & T160

American influence on Triumph during the Trident's life has become legendary: that original Daytona entry, upping the 650cc twins to 750s... and the Hurricane. In 1969, dealers in the States were still reeling from their first reaction to the Ogle-designed triples, which gave Don Brown (then BSA Inc Vice-President) the idea of a factory custom – a niche market bike.

Not everyone likes factory customs, mainly because of the many examples which consist of high-rise bars and some extra chrome. But the Hurricane was different – the attention to detail transforming the 'middle-aged' Trident. Above all, it had style. In short, it was arguably the best ever factory custom, with a genuinely new look which acknowledged the trends of the time.

As with the Trident, it took years to make the short step from prototype to production. Craig Vetter, the young bike stylist from Illinois, took only a few months to transform the triple's appearance. Working on a standard Rocket Three (he was believed to have preferred the BSA engine – its sloping cylinders were aesthetically parallel to the frame downtubes) he soon established the flowing single tank/seat unit as the bike's centrepiece.

Left
Two of Alistair Laurie's radically lightened Tridents – none of the bikes he built were the same. One has Borrani wire wheels, the other mag SMACs, but both use Rob North-type frames using Reynolds 531 tubing

Right
Slippery Sam at the 1976 TT. Riders Alex George and Percy Tait (winners on Sam the previous year) were entered by NVT for the ten lap production race. Sadly they crashed, which marked the end of triple domination on the Island

Overleaf
Ray Pickrell, one of Sam's happy TT partners, racing a 750 Trident in 1969. (Photo courtesy Mick Walker)

The three cylinders were emphasised by three chrome pipes sweeping out of the engine to three upswept megaphones – how different from the factory bikes, which tried to make out they were twins! It wasn't all totally new, but there were pleasing nods to current and past styles which added to the appeal; the narrow tank was very late-sixties Triumph; the modestly raked front forks acknowledged the chopper craze. There were also innumerable details, like extended finning on the cylinder head, and polished hubs, which added to the overall impact. The result was a masterpiece, looking lithe and light in a way that the standard triple wasn't. Vetter knew the importance of giving the engine centre stage, and of allowing 'light gaps' in the profile. It was also around 50 lb lighter than standard, which was good news.

In September 1969, Vetter showed the prototype to BSA Inc, who were so impressed that they packed it straight off to England. A year later, *Cycle World* were permitted a cover story detailing the new bike,

Above
Special engine cover to accommodate the magneto drive, polished and machined. Inside, the engine had a 1-litre conversion. Both engine and bike were built in 1977, just as the factory Trident was becoming history

Left
Beautifully finished, acres of polished alloy, massive 'silencer' (an optimistic description) – the ultimate cafe racer?

Left

Neil Payne's Hurricane on a rain-sodden Dartmoor, far from the sun-soaked Californian highways for which it was intended

Above

Still on Dartmoor, this was why photographers tended to concentrate on the righthand side of the Hurricane – the three upswept megaphones made a dramatic statement

but it wasn't until mid-1972 that it finally went into production. This was not entirely due to Meriden/Small Heath laziness; the company was collapsing at the time and had undertaken to build the Hurricane exactly as Vetter designed it. This involved, among other things, special casting for the wide fin head. Gearing was lower as well, which, with the lighter weight, produced stunning acceleration – though high speed stability and cruising was somewhat hampered by the high, wide bars. The Hurricane didn't last long on the price lists, but then it was only ever intended as a limited edition image-maker. Only around 1,100 were made (the exact figure depends on who you believe). It is doubtful that they turned over much of a profit, despite the £200 price premium over a standard Trident.

Collapse & Hope

Even as late as its first official showing to US dealers, the Hurricane wore BSA badges. That it was sold as a Triumph was purely down to 'trouble at t'mill'. Patchy quality, the sheer waste at Umberslade and throughout the company (as well as numerous other problems) led to a sudden lurch into losses. After years of profits, the company lost £3.3 million in 1971.

One fall-out was the decision to stop making BSA-badged bikes. Small Heath's 5,400 workforce was slashed to 1,500 in just six weeks (those who remained continued to build Trident engines); the Rocket Three was dropped and, of course, the Hurricane became a Triumph. There was also a new board, headed by industrialist Lord Shawcross, which included Bert Hopwood as engineering chief. Despite the problems (massive debts, stocks of unsold bikes, Meriden's industrial relations) there was genuine hope that this could be the beginning of a new age.

Hopwood, Hele and the design team devised a plan for product revival, which was to culminate in an all-new range of bikes in 1976. Another Bert Hopwood brainchild, it was to have used the modular concept from a 200cc single to 1 litre V5. If Lord Shawcross could reduce losses and secure government backing, it might be possible. In theory, the old triples and twins just had to be kept fresh enough to last a few more years.

Above

It started life as a BSA, but was a Triumph by the time it lumbered into production. You could have any colour you wanted, incidentally, as long as it was orange with yellow flashes

Right

It's not obvious here, but the Hurricane had its own big fin head, to make the engine as much of a styling feature as everything else. It was typical of Vetter's attention to detail and certainly added to the overall impact

Above

The Hurricane looked a bit bare from this side, certainly a complete transformation from the original – the high rise bars were standard of course, as were Borrani alloy rims

Left

The conical hubs were one of the few Hurricane parts to remain unchanged. The prototype's Ceriani forks were swapped for lengthened BSA/Triumph stanchions on production bikes

Now based at Kitt's Green, the team's main weapon, long before the
T160 appeared, was the electric start Thunderbird III. This bike has been
been ascribed various engine sizes over the years, though 830cc is the most
common. Basically a long-stroke version of the standard triple, it boosted
power to 67bhp at 8,300rpm, and gave impressive mid-range torque.
According to Norman Hyde, it was little changed apart from different stud
positions and longer barrel and pushrods. Had it appeared as planned in
1973, this modernised triple might have been able to make a difference.
As it was, the Meriden blockade was enough to have it cancelled.

There was another attempt to modernise the triples. As with the twins,
adding an overhead cam could (it was thought) usefully extend their life.
It actually reached the prototype stage, with a toothed rubber belt running
up the timing side to a single overhead cam. This was driven by a shaft in
the old exhaust camshaft position, while another shaft in place of the inlet
cam drove the cb points. Yet, like the ohc twin, despite experimentation
with various cam forms and profiles, it just wouldn't give any more power
than the pushrod triple. There were also the 'Trisolastic' (a triple engine
in Norton Commando Isolastic chassis) and 'Quadrant' (simply a triple
with an extra cylinder tacked on).

Meanwhile, the T150 was not having an easy time of things either.
When the Meriden blockade was set up in September 1973, Trident

production stopped. The political background has been well documented elsewhere but, briefly, the government of the day had agreed to put in some money to save the bike industry, but only if BSA/Triumph merged with the apparently successful Norton under Dennis Poore. They agreed, although the resulting NVT had Poore as Chairman. It was Poore's sudden announcement that Meriden was to close which sparked off the blockade from which Meriden eventually emerged as a workers' co-op – and actually continued to survive for a further eight years.

Nevertheless, all this meant no more Tridents for the time being, since relations had been broken between Small Heath (where the engines were built) and Meriden (cycle parts and assembly). After six months, NVT did manage to restart production of the T150 at Small Heath; some of the tools and drawings were still at Meriden, and had to be expensively remade. Dennis Poore estimated the delay and extra work had cost NVT half a

Above
Brian Gilling at speed on his Hurricane. The styling that looked so good didn't do much for handling – the bike was accused of top heaviness and suspect high speed steering by testers

Right
The T160 engine was a bit of a hybrid, with the BSA tilted cylinders and Triumph gearbox cover. The overdue Lucas electric start actually worked quite well

Left
*T160s had their own downpipe
arrangement, splitting into four pipes
rather than two – a fashion statement?
Nice sunflower yellow colour scheme*

Above
*A more modern look console for the
mid-'70s incorporating the ignition key
and warning lights. Rubber-mounted
NVT instruments*

million pounds, but it was worth his while to persevere with the Trident.
Demand for the bike was high at the time, and production was soon up to
200 a week. In this form, with a lower compression ratio and minor
gearing changes, the T150 lasted another year in its new home, until it was
eventually succeeded by its short-lived replacement – the T160.

T160 – Last of the Old Guard

The T160, just like all the other old Tridents, was a mixture of near-
brilliance with annoying details. It looked better than the T150, handled
more securely, had an electric start and disc brakes at both ends; yet it was
slower and thirstier than the old bike, would still leak oil and show little
patches of vibration.

More than a last-ditch facelift, the last Trident was substantially
changed. There was a new frame, based on that of the works production

racers – longer and lower than before, with longer swinging arm and
shorter forks. The engine used the old Rocket III system of tilted
cylinders, mainly to make room for the starter, but with the added benefit
of better weight distribution. Internally, little was changed, with things
like ball-bearing tappet adjusters and steel capped pushrods, though the
primary drive did change to a bigger duplex chain.

As to the Lucas starter – "a mere ten or twelve years late", said *Cycle
World* – this had originally been mooted as early as 1971, and the clutch-
driving arrangement had been laid out by Norman Hyde in 1973.
However, industrial troubles, as ever, had caused delay. There was a new
3-4-2 exhaust system, this was in place partly to deal with noise
regulations and also to create the impression of four downpipes and four
cylinders. To meet the latest American laws, the gearchange moved to the
left-hand side.

Above
*Tim Smithell's high mileage T160 in non-standard colours and twin disc front end,
but showing the longer, lower look of the last Tridents*

Right
*Pete Cornock's 1975 T160 was re-imported from Minnesota with only 6,000 miles
showing. Poor sales of the T160 in the US had been one of the vital factors in the
demise of the NVT triple.. It is basically standard, with the Cherokee Red finish
with which many models left the factory*

In fact, the T160 embodied over 200 changes and, by all accounts, most of them were worthwhile. Most importantly, the styling was right at last. The only obvious change was the fuel tank, which managed to combine a good 4.8 gallons with classic slimline Triumph looks. Being longer and lower than the T150 helped too. It made the Trident, perhaps for the first time, look like a real Meriden bike. (Ironic, as most were built at Small Heath and the last batch of all in Andover.)

Despite extra weight (the T160 was quoted as a hefty 503lb), every single road test was extremely enthusiastic about the handling – better than the old Trident, than any Japanese bike, and well up with the Italians. Yet it was a pity that most of them found it slower than before (*Cycle World* managed 109mph, and *Motor Cycle* only scraped the ton with an upright rider), and thought the riding position, with its forward-set footrests, was no better. Perhaps the real stumbling block was the price. No road tester could fail to point out that the T160 cost £1,215,

Above

A Trident makes an unusual chair puller, and this one even has solo gearing, but a Steib in matching colours looks good

Right

Like many well-used Tridents, this one has some out of sight mods to improve its practicality – Boyer electronic ignition, 180W alternator, Hyde heavy duty chain, twin disc conversion

Above

Being a Production Racer, Sam had relatively minor mods. Mild tuning produced around 75bhp at 8,500rpm, there were Fontana drum brakes (later changed for discs), a Quaife five-speed gearbox and aluminium rims

Right

Slippery Sam's TT story is well known, but for the record: 1970, 4th place at 94.14mph, ridden by Eddie Dow; 1971, 1st at 100.07mph, Ray Pickrell; 1972, 1st at 100mph, Ray Pickrell; 1973, 1st at 95.62mph, Tony Jeffries; 1974, 1st at 99.72mph, Mick Grant; 1975, 1st at 99.60mph, Dave Croxford and Alex George

Left
*Les Williams and his reborn Trident,
the Legend. This T160 based bike, with
its big aluminium tank and superb
finish, is typical*

Above
*The idea behind the Legend was to
continue development of the Trident in
an evolutionary way, by the man who
knew more about its foibles than just
about anyone else*

well up on the old bike and over £200 more than a Honda 750. The story
was much the same in the States, where Tridents were being heavily
discounted to get them moving.

The end finally came when one of NVT's suppliers (owed £23,000)
petitioned for settlement. Although the company was able to keep going in
a small way, making spares, it meant the end of bike production at Small
Heath. For the time being, the Triumph Trident was dead.

The Alistair Laurie Tridents

Scotsman Alistair Laurie built a lot of bikes – cafe racers from north of
the border. Every year he would go to the Isle Of Man, and every year he
would leave with plenty of cash in his pockets, having sold another of his
hand-built bikes. The Tridents shown here were lower, slimmer, faster and
more radically lightened than any other bike he had built before. In fact

they were comparatively tiny. Weighing just 129kg, with a seat height of a mere 25 inches, they measured little more than 15 inches across the engine.

Everything was pared to the absolute minimum – the fairing was a 1oz fibre glass lay-up, thin as a potato crisp, and the seat was just a single sheet of vinyl. The seat unit and three gallon tank were hand beaten by Alistair from 16 gauge aluminium.

Wheels were Eric Offenstadt magnesium alloy, machined by Alistair and finished off with a pair of home-brewed brake discs. Alistair made them at a local forge, using scrap aluminium alloy from Lo-Ex car pistons. The weight saving paid off, and the front wheel disc and magnesium alloy Lockheed caliper together weighed a surprising 30lb less than similar set-ups on previous home-made machines. The engine, naturally enough, was far from standard. Enlarged to 870cc, the barrels were bored out to accept

Above

Ex-BSA man Graham Saunders was responsible for the glassfibre, and Des Roberts of Raven paintwork finished it off

Right

One of the advantages of bespoke production is that colour preferences can be included – deep glossy metallics were a later addition

Left

Les wanted to give the Legend a completely different look to the Trident, and succeeded. It looks neater, more compact and somehow more modern

Above

Apart from the oil pressure gauge, this is standard Trident equipment

Hepolite pistons which were machined from blocks of alloy. Again, weight saving was all, and the pistons were just 130 thou thick at the valve pockets. American Morris cams cost £80, and ensured the engine came on song at 5,500rpm and stayed there through to 10,000.

In fact nothing escaped the fight against flab. Everywhere you look, there are weight saving holes – in the mudguards, bolts, spindles, clips, nuts, discs, the seat and the gears. Less conventional were the chrome-plated plastic bath plugs for the mag-bodied carb stacks. Or the police bafflers in the silencers, operated by a nylon-lined piano cable wire from a lever on the bars. Geared for 180mph, yet weighing the same as a contemporary 250, Alistair Laurie Tridents were extraordinary.

Left

The primary drive had to change when Renold stopped producing duplex chains – so it was back to T150 style triplex

Above

None of the Legends were super tuned. Just an internally cleaned up head, electronic ignition and very careful assembly by Arthur Jakeman, made them smoother, quieter and more reliable than any regular Small Heath-built triple

The Les Williams Tridents

Two men who had worked on the Meriden Tridents maintained the connection for years after production ceased. Norman Hyde made a living out of tuning (his 850 and 1000 long-stroke kits were well known), while Les Williams concentrated on restyling and updating.

Les wasn't a Midlands man, but born and brought up near Brecon. National Service in the Royal Signals meant work as a despatch rider ("everyone put down 'despatch rider' when they joined up", he later recalled), followed by a coveted place in the Signals' motorcycle display team. That in turn meant a fitters' course at Meriden, and when demob time came, he was offered a job in the Service Department.

He liked it, and stayed, progressing through the Experimental Department to take charge of the racing effort from 1969. The inevitable redundancies followed – from Triumph in late 1973, and NVT in '75,

Left

Demand for the Legend outstripped supply, but ultimately production was limited by their hand-built nature, which was how the customers wanted it

Above

Trevor Gleadhall and his re-interpretation of the Legend – the Renegade

but Les found himself busier than ever. He had bought all the racing spares after leaving NVT, using the stock to start his own business. Things soon changed when dealers began clamouring for replicas of Slippery Sam, as this veteran of the Isle Of Man had just won the TT yet again. Mike Jackson (still working as NVT's Sales Manager at the time) suggested that Les take on the work.

A prototype was built up in the garage – with a new seat and tank unit, rear sets and clip-ons – and sent down to the Bike Show. The response was immediate, with 47 orders pouring in straight away. "It was impossible" said Les, "I was working all night". These were all new bikes of course, but as the word got round, existing Trident owners began to bring their bikes up for the Slippery Sam treatment – it was the makings of a long-term business. The local council apparently thought so too and, after three months, voiced an objection to such intensive use of the Williams garage.

Above

*Like Les, Trevor didn't want to boost
performance too much, but to make the
Trident more practical as 1990s
transport – electrics are fully updated*

Right

*The family resemblance to Legend is
clear. If this was a Honda, the styling
would be 'retro'. As a Trident, it's a
clean update but there are also plenty
of nods to the past*

Left

Big aluminium tank, as on the Legend, and T160 base – five speeds and electric start seem to be in keeping with the more modern image

Above

Few owners spending this amount of money on a Trident would do without an oil pressure gauge, despite the warning light

Undeterred, he enlisted the help of Arthur Jakeman, rented a workshop in Kenilworth and got down to work. Although spares were always the business mainstay, there was a steady trickle of Tridents arriving in Kenilworth. In all, 32 Slippery Sam replicas were built. In '84, the Legend appeared, which was really an updated version of the same thing. The formula was the same – rearsets, rounded styling and a single seat. They were rarely tuned (though most bikes had some minor head work), but always had electronic ignition, a high priority mod for the old triples. The realities of the motorcycle component industry meant German Magura switchgear, Italian dampers and Spanish rims, as much of the British component industry (as opposed to spares) was dead by this time. The bikes were hand-built, and had a ready market among the wealthier enthusiasts, though later machines did use British Hagon dampers. About sixty were made before Trevor Gleadall bought most of the L.P. Williams business, on Les's retirement. Trevor, in turn, developed his own version of Legend, the Renegade. There are some changes, but the spirit is the same, and it is still possible to order one from the works in Common Lane, Kenilworth.

Above
Big twin leading shoe drum replaces standard disc

Left
The solo seat looks almost big enough for two, but the lack of pillion pegs betrays its real purpose

Right
Norman Hyde's well known logo graces the tank of a Harris 3 – note the just visible carburettor bellmouths

Above

Owner Neil Townsend uses his Harris on the road and competes successfully on track – complete reliability in both cases

Left

The Harrier is basically a frame kit to suit any Small Heath triple engine. This one is based on a 1974 T150 enlarged to 900cc and producing 80bhp. The owner reckons it has more torque than an 851 Ducati

Left
Twin Cibie headlights give Neil Townsend's bike a genuine cafe racer look, or is it an endurance racer?

Above
The Harrier 3 uses a Harris frame specifically designed for the triple. It comes as a kit of bits, which includes Marzocchi 42mm forks, Koni Dial-A-Ride rear shocks and the innumerable bits and pieces needed to make a complete bike

New Beginnings

When the remains of the Meriden co-op were sold off in late 1983, the press and motorcycling public seemed far more concerned with Les Harris than John Bloor. Both were businessmen who wanted to build Triumphs – the difference was that Harris had leased the rights to make the Bonneville for five years, while Bloor had bought the Triumph name and manufacturing rights lock, stock and barrel. He even had the right to build Meriden's 900cc Phoenix if he chose. But the emphasis on Les Harris was understandable – his plans to build Bonnies were far more public than those of Bloor, who gave little indication of what he was doing.

It was a sensible silence, which the new company maintained almost up until the final launch in 1990. More to the point, it allowed them to take their time, thus ensuring that the bikes were right before they went on sale. This approach, a considerable contrast to the old company's 'firefighting' model development, proved to be a good one.

History, and the UK motorcycle press, has not been kind to the frequent attempts to revive the British bike industry (or rather, modest ventures by enthusiasts which have been portrayed as such). There was Meriden's long-awaited water-cooled twin, the Phoenix; the even longer story of the Norton rotary (ten years of development followed by ten years of limited production); and the Hesketh saga. The differences between these sorry tales and those of the new Triumph, and the reasons why they failed whereas Triumph succeeded, would fill a book. Suffice to say that with John Bloor, Triumph had a sole financial backer with the means and patience to see a fully developed bike to market – no shareholders champing at the bit, no scraping around for money.

Modular Revival

Development proceeded from 1984 in Coventry, while the following year work started on a brand-new factory at Hinckley, Leicestershire. Odd snippets came out now and then – an engine had done 500 hours on the testbed; a disguised prototype was seen at MIRA; even the modernised Triumph logo made front page news in MCN! When the bikes finally appearer (at the Cologne Show in 1990) they certainly made an impact. Not just one new bike, but six; 750 and 900 triples, with fours of 1000 and 1200cc, sports, sports-touring and unfaired bikes. Within the company they were coded T375 (750), T309 (900), T310 (1000) and T312 (1200).

Right
One early criticism was the slightly nondescript looking engine. Triumph's response was a choice of grey crinkle finish (Sprint, Trophy) or black (everything else)

It was the modular concept, which Bert Hopwood had such hopes for twenty years earlier, that made this all possible. All four engines shared the same 76mm bore, but with a stroke of 55mm (750 and 1000), or 65mm (900/1200). Using the same bore (though with different pistons to allow alternative compression ratios) meant both the 750/900 and 1000/1200 could share a cylinder head each. All bikes used the same steel backbone frame; it wasn't up to the minute, but relatively cheap, and it did allow different bodywork according to model. Naturally enough, costs were minimised, and so ease of production was maximised.

There were those who accused Triumph of producing a Kawasaki GPZ clone. Certainly there was nothing new about the engine, but it was more a collection of typical Japanese practice than a copy of one design. Watercooled of course, with four valves per cylinder and twin overhead cams driven by hy-vo chain running up the right-hand side. There were

Water cooling demands a temperature gauge, but otherwise there's little more information on this Trident console than the old one

Tony Pettit on his '91 Trophy 900. With his past of many British bikes he probably wasn't the typical customer — most had come over from Japanese or European machines

wet liners (not a Kawasaki feature) and valve adjustment by shims (which owed more to Yamaha). But what really set the new Triumphs apart was the triple. Yamaha, Kawasaki and Suzuki had all built three-cylinder bikes in the past, but all had stopped making them by 1990. Both the 750 and 900 used 120° cranks, just like the old Trident, but added a balance shaft for good measure. Running at engine speed, this would help counteract vibration, and the company claimed a balance factor of almost 100%, which later road tests seemed to confirm.

Primary drive was by straight-cut gears, with fine tolerances to eliminate whine; all bikes got the same six-speed gearbox and wet multiplate clutch. There were some signs of compromise, forced by the modular concept. In order to be stiff enough to cope with the 125bhp 1200 (and future power hikes), the backbone chassis had to be bigger and heavier than was strictly necessary for the smaller engined bikes. This, however, was the only really

significant change. For minimal outlay, Triumph had a complete range of bikes for the 750+ market, all ready to sell within about six months of the first launch.

It was a cautious approach, with no wild innovations, but one which made sense. The new Triumphs showed proven technology and absolute reliability; they had to be competitive, but they didn't have to surpass the Japanese in every single area. The name alone, it has to be said, accounted for much of their appeal.

The new company was extremely keen to distance itself from the old – only a few ex-Meriden men went to work at Hinckley, and new and old bikes had only the name in common – yet it did realise the sense of making use of old, respected names. So the unfaired bikes, sold with 750 and 900 triples, were the new Tridents. Daytona was chosen for the faired sportsters (four cylinders only at first), and Trophy (900 and 1200) for the tourers.

Above
Road tests of those early Hinckley Triumphs were just a little taken aback. The bikes were better than anyone had predicted

Right
The Trophy 900 in its original dark blue form. For many, this was the most practical bike in the range – fast enough, but cheaper and less heavy than the 1200

Cynics Surprised

The cynicism of the motorcycle press was understandable. Time and time again, they had seen big promises come to nothing. An example is the Hesketh – test rides on the original handbuilt prototypes brought some great superlatives, but the production bikes turned out to be underdeveloped, over-priced and (in sales terms) over-ambitious. Would the same be true of the new Triumphs? When those first UK road tests emerged in the spring of 1991, it very soon became clear that this time everything was going to be all right.

Phil West wrote in May 1991's *Bike*: "Top speed? 152mph, with the potential for much, much more. Gearbox? Probably the best I've ever used. All-over engine performance? Astounding. Handling? Yes. Comfort? Yes. Stickers? Yes, and all in English. No Japanese, no German, no kidding. This is the bike that changes views of Brit bikes forever. This competes...

Above

The Trophy was supposed to be Triumph's tourer, but some early tests thought the riding position a little too sporting – repositioned bars and footrests soon followed

Right

Detail of Trophy fairing, showing engine peephole – this clever styling ploy served to break up an otherwise slab-sided fairing

Left

Japanese Nissan brakes were standard
across the Hinckley range; fifteen years
after the old Trident, the UK
components industry was gone too

Right

The six-speed gearbox was another
modular building block – 750 and 900
Tridents even used the same length
chain, despite different gearbox
sprockets

with the best." He was actually writing about the Trophy 1200; rather
than launch all six at once, Triumph adopted a rolling programme which
saw the flagship appear early in May and the Daytona 1000 in mid-month.
The original intention had been to follow up with the first triples (Trophy
900 and Daytona 750) in early June and the Tridents later the same
month. However, they were late, but by early autumn the complete range
of bikes was out there and selling. The significance of those early road tests
was that everyone was genuinely surprised that the Triumphs were, for
once, pretty good. Although the 1200 fours impressed everyone with their
sheer torque, it was the long-stroke triple that really got writers going,
particularly in the case of the Trident...

"This engine is utterly awesome, towing the Trident on from less than
2,000rpm right through to the redline with the kind of response to throttle
and clutch which pales into insignificance many so-called sports bikes and
might even give a few similarly sized legends of the industry such as the
Ninja or the Ducati 900SS a beating in the midrange too." (*Fast Bike*). It
soon became clear that the 900 would become the testers' (and customers')
favourite Triumph engine. The noise it made was striking; despite water
cooling and massive silencers, it still possessed that distinctive high revs
wail that only a triple can make. Its smoothness was also outstanding; only
one balancer shaft was needed, as opposed to two for the fours.

Most of all, bike testers seemed to have rediscovered torque. Perhaps,
after a steady diet of ever-revvier race replicas, the new Trident seemed
like a breath of fresh air. Not that ex-Jota and old Trident-owning

Left
Switchgear, instruments and tank were the same whichever early Bloor Triumph you bought. Flat topped, tank-bag friendly fuel tank was useful

Above
The basic Trident 750 in 1994 spec, which brought silver wheels and black engine, but kept the popular British Racing Green

Mark Williams needed reminding: "But like the old Trident this engine – with its 120° crank and hefty flywheel – produces a surge of power from deep down in the bowels of its rev range and keeps it coming, like some cunningly plumbed tidal wave, 'till well past the red line. Personally, I love four-stroke triples for their inherent abundance of torque, and the new Trident is up there with the Laverda Jota in the superleague of triple treats." (*Motorcycle International*, November 1991). There were some grumbles about the fuel consumption (the Trident 900 often averaged the mid-thirties), but really they couldn't have hoped for a better reception.

In comparison to the impact of the engine, the rest of the bike seemed a little insignificant. Nevertheless, the Trident's handling came in for particular praise, which was surprising given the overall impression that all the new Triumphs were big, tall and heavy. It was really a combination of the tall engine (due to the big sump, said some) and backbone frame,

which added height on top of, rather than around, the engine. There were
a few complaints about paddling the bikes round at walking pace, but most
seem to agree that once under way, the potential top-heaviness didn't
materialise. At least, that was true of the Tridents and Trophys. The
Daytona, being ostensibly a sportster, didn't too so well, simply because
more was expected. It was up against the race-replicas, with their top-end
tuned engines and alloy wrap-round frames. Instead, the Daytona was
labelled a 'sports tourer' by the press; unfortunately, Triumph didn't sell
very many as a result.

There were also mixed feelings about the short-stroke triple, the 750.
Motorcycle International put a Daytona up against a VFR750 Honda, and
criticised the Triumph for having a peaky engine with little mid-range
housed in a heavy bike. Strangely, however, when *Bike* tested both Trident
and Daytona 750s, they made a point of praising the mid-range power (by
750 standards). Wherever the truth lay, no-one could deny that the short-
stroke Triumph engines just didn't have the torque of the others. And the
message must have got through to the punters – Trident 900s were soon
outselling the 750s by around five to one.

But that didn't really matter. The ecstatic reception of the long-stroke
engines (the triple especially), made up for minor niggles. The bikes were
selling well too, at least in the UK. At first, the official line was that
Germany was the major target market. It wasn't just that it was big; it was
felt that if you could sell to the Germans, you could sell to anyone. On top
of that, their TUV tests were acknowledged to be the toughest in Europe.

TUV-approved Triumphs would be that much easier to gain acceptance elsewhere. In Britain, however, the primary aim was not to outsell BMW. It didn't happen like that, and Germany was an early setback for Triumph. In fact, in 1992, Germany took less than 300 bikes whereas France bought 480 and Britain 1,200. The German episode was one reason why Triumph failed to make its target of 6,000 sales in '92; less than 5,000 bikes were sold. Though in the UK, many people seemed delighted to have a modern British bike to buy. There were even stories of unsold export bikes being brought back to meet demand at home as early as September 1991; British sales had overtaken those in Germany. Indicative of the huge UK interest was the number of dealer applications; two-thirds of all dealers applied for a Triumph franchise. Their enthusiasm was justified by a launch and trouble-free early life. A batch of faulty head gaskets was the only serious teething trouble, and it seemed that everyone could breathe a sigh of relief.

Above
Hinckley evidently thought the Trident 900 needed distancing from its little brother, so brought in some new colour schemes with more than a hint of T160

Right
The early Daytona 750 looked a bit too Japanese, and both 750 and 1000 short-stroke engines were always compared unfavourably with long-stroke cousins

Developments

That Triumph would broaden its range was inevitable, and the modular concept made it relatively easy to do so. Alternative bodywork, with a few tweaks to engine and gearing produced something completely different, or at least one that seemed completely different anyway. Yet there was another reason; the big bike market was diversifying into several niches – sports, race replica, tourer, enduro, retro – and Triumph needed to cover as many of these as possible to maximise market share. Things had been different back in the old Trident days, when riders had a choice of one.

This trend really started in the 1980s, when Japanese sports bikes got more extreme – the first race replicas. This was mirrored in other niches – as the Paris-Dakar Rally grew in popularity, so did the number of big enduro-style bikes on the market (a trend started by, of all people, arch-conservative BMW). Then as the '80s ended, the retro appeared on a wave of horribly inevitable 1970s nostalgia – no fairing, air-cooled engines (or air-cooled styling at least) and rounded tanks. Triumph's unfaired Trident didn't quite fit into this category. Its engine was too obviously liquid-cooled; its styling too much like a modern bike minus fairing.

It would be nice to say that the Trident was a cunning re-interpretation of an old style, rather than a slavish copy based on nostalgia. It is more likely to have been something of an afterthought. The retro boom only really got going while the Hinckley bikes were in their final development stage, and the Trident's styling really betrays it as a faired bike without the fairing. But even if it was an eleventh hour reaction to the latest trend, the cheapest Triumph scored well with both punters and press. After a year or so the engine acquired a black finish (which made it look more like a motorcycle engine and less like some anonymous lump), and ugly cooling hoses were covered up. But behind the scenes, more radical plans were under way.

Right and overleaf

The Paul Taylor three-cylinder Laverda racer had come to the end of its useful racing life. Where else to look for a triple replacement than Triumph? John Bloor provided the engine and the Saxon semi-works racer won in July 1994 at Zeltweg in Austria, the first international Triumph victory for 19 years, Alan Cathcart at the helm. The BEARS racer tubular ally space frame with semi-stressed engine weighed in at 162kgs dry, not far off the 155kg limit planned for 3 pot Superbike

Good to Torque: Tiger & Sprint

The Tiger 900 wasn't the first big off-road Triumph. The last days of Meriden had seen the emergence of the Tiger Trail 750, basically a detuned Bonneville with knobbly tyres and a few other sops for off-road use. These didn't sell in great numbers, though these were the days when a bike with off-road styling was expected to be the genuine article. By the time the new Tiger came along, the market had changed, and many riders were looking for something which looked like a real 'mud muncher', but was really a fast, comfy touring bike.

Yamaha's Super Tenere, Honda's Africa Twin and the latest off-road BMW (the R100 GS) were all cashing in. It was not for nothing that John Bloor described the Tiger as a street bike equivalent to a Range Rover – it was an admission that the latest Triumph would rarely get its tyres muddy.

Triumph Sprint 900, an excellent example of Hinckley's mix and match strategy – it was basically a Trident with a half fairing

In 1994, the Tiger 900 was Triumph's most radical departure yet — bodywork, exhaust and engine tune were all unique to that model

Work started in late 1991, centring on the new plastic bodywork. The big 5.3 gallon fuel tank was made of nylon, and shaped to wrap around the stanchions to shift weight forward. It was blended into a twin headlight upper fairing, with 'Tiger' scrawled across the whole assembly. There were other off-road styling cues, such as a bashplate, and Motad helped design an upswept exhaust. It wasn't all cosmetic though, and the by-now familiar 900 triple was detuned, just in case the Tiger rider ever did venture off-road. New camshafts with lower lift and less duration brought power down from 100PS to 85PS at 8,000rpm. Peak torque was also down marginally, but there was a much more even spread, with only a 5 % difference in output between 2,500 and 8,500rpm.

The press loved it, with the important proviso that it never be taken for more than the most gentle off-road excursion. Bikes like the BMW GS or Cagiva Elefant were either lighter, more manageable — or both.

But it was on tarmac that the Tiger scored. Even in detuned form, the triple made it the fastest bike of its type (top speed was over 130mph whereas a BMW could barely manage 100), while the almost flat torque curve produced honking acceleration from around 2,000rpm. It really underlined what was fast becoming a Hinckley triple byword – massive mid-range torque. Unfortunately, the Tiger was also a good example of another Hinckley characteristic – poor fuel consumption. Right from the very first road tests, triples had averaged figures in the mid-thirties. It didn't affect the Trophy so much, with its relatively good aerodynamics, but a Trident or Tiger could easily dip below 35mpg (one Tiger tester even recorded 28mpg on one run into a strong wind). Treated gently, they could creep up to 45-50mpg, and Japanese bikes of the same performance weren't a great deal better. Nevertheless, it was a disappointing result for a supposedly relaxed and torquey engine.

By Hinckley Triumph standards, the Tiger was pretty radical, but the Trident Sprint was far more familiar. Introduced at around the same time, it was basically a Trident with a half-fairing, a response to Trident owners who said they wanted a fairing but not a Trophy. Like the Tiger, it came only with the 900 triple (though in 98bhp Trident tune of course) which had become far and away Triumph's best selling engine – three-cylinder bikes made up around 85-90 % of Hinckley production by this time. Most of those were 900s, as the 750 had been relegated purely as an entry-level Trident. Apart from the fairing, the Sprint also acquired the Daytona's four-piston calipers, as did the Trophy that year. The two-piston ones had been criticised as a bit marginal for such big heavy bikes, and it seemed Triumph listened to criticism.

Sportsters: Daytona, Speed Triple, Super III

One bike which got a less than ecstatic reception was the original Daytona. Ostensibly the sporting Hinckley Triumph, it lacked the torquey long stroke engines which everyone was raving about, and there were mutterings that it just wasn't sporty enough and looked too Japanese.

Within a year it was dead, replaced by new Daytonas which looked very different but, of course, had all the familiar Hinckley bits underneath. In went the 900 triple, in its usual 98PS Trident/Trophy tune (plus a 147PS tuned 1200). There was more rounded bodywork and bright, bold colours. The bike was transformed, thanks yet again to the 900 triple. What it didn't do was transform the Daytona into a light, flickable sportster like the Honda FireBlade. Climb onto one for the first time, and it feels like what it is: a big, heavy motorcycle. Despite the lower seat height for 1993, it's still impossible for anyone of below average height to plant both feet firmly on the ground, and the bars are quite a stretch away. Naturally none of this is too noticeable once under way, and what could seem simply intimidating is saved by the user-friendly engine. It's docile and tractable, pulling smoothly from less than 2,000rpm, and with rapid acceleration regardless of gear. Which leads one back to the conclusion of the first Daytona road tests – it's more sports-tourer than race replica.

The Daytona was aimed at a familiar market niche, but the Speed Triple was different. Basically a Daytona minus fairing, it was (said the ads) a modern cafe racer, all raw thrills and power. It did well in the road tests, and not just because the 900 triple worked its customary charm. Real trouble had been taken with the details to make it look right – black finished engine, white-faced chrome-rimmed instruments – the Speed Triple managed to convey a muscular appeal different from any other Triumph. A real factory street fighter.

Launched alongside the Speed Triple, at a show in Paris in the autumn of 1993, was the Daytona Super III. Hinckley was nothing if not realistic,

Right
Even the Triumph patent badge reappeared – it seemed as if the more confident Hinckley became, the happier it was to underline the link with Meriden

Left

Detuning to 85bhp brought a much wider spread of torque to the Tiger, just in case the rider really did venture off tarmac

Above

Minor styling changes made a big difference to the engine. The black and silver finish was preferable to the big metal-coloured lump in the first bikes

and knew that the standard Daytonas were too heavy and not quite fast enough to be treated as out and out sportsters. Hence the Super III, which made a determined effort to reduce weight and increase power. Silencers and mudguards were of carbon-fibre, and Cosworth produced a pressure cast cylinder head and crankcases which reduced engine weight by a substantial 2.5kg.

Higher compression pistons (12:1 rather than 10.6) revised inlets, and valve gear helped boost power to 113bhp at 9,500rpm. Torque was up slightly at 65.6lb/ft, but at a much higher than normal 8,500rpm. And there were new six-piston brake calipers, made specially for the bike by a firm whose bread and butter work was parts for Formula One cars. There was, of course, a price tag to match, and the Super III was announced at £9,699, which was £1,500 more than a Daytona 900.

It was a pity that both a Fire Blade and Kawasaki ZX-9R had more

TYRE INFORMATION
FRONT TYRE FITMENT, SIZE, BRAND
1) MICHELIN TS6X 110/80 R19
2) PIRELLI MT60 100/90 -19
WARNING - DO NOT MIX TYRE BRANDS EG. BRAND 1) FRONT WITH BRAND 2)
COLD TYRE PRESSURES

REAR TYRE FITMENT, SIZE, BRAND
1) MICHELIN TS6X 140/80 R17
2) PIRELLI MT60 140/80 - 17

COLD TYRE PRESSURES	FRONT			REAR	
	KG/CM²	KPa	LB/IN²		KG/CM²
MICHELIN	2.1	210	30		2.3
PIRELLI	2.0	200	28.5		2.3

power and could top 160mph against the Triumph's 145. They were cheaper, had quicker handling and used less fuel in the process. Of course, the traditional Hinckley strengths were all there in the Super III – tremendous mid-range and tractability, good build quality, that lovely triple howl – but it was clear that to really compete with the race replicas, an alloy perimeter frame was needed. Writing this in 1994, there's no sign of one coming from Hinckley. Maybe next year...

Made in England: Inside the Factory

Turn off a wind-swept A5 and you are confronted by a fairly prosaic, humdrum industrial estate. The factory isn't quite as anonymous as it used to be – giant 'Triumph' logos now grace the frontage – but there's nothing else to tell you that this is the home of the British bike renaissance. Even now, the estate map board only refers to 'J.S. Bloor' –

Left

This was really the second generation Daytona, with its bright reds and yellows and big bold graphics. Despite the looks, the engine was still in 98bhp Trident tune

Above

Smoothed out fairing round the two 60/55w halogens – Pimento Red, Racing Yellow and Barracuda Blue were the choices

Overleaf

The Daytona 900 – a marriage of the 900 triple with Triumph's sportster – was far better received than the old one

Above

That old bike book cliché, "this is the view other riders got..." etc doesn't really apply, as the Daytona simply wasn't as quick as the race replicas

Right

The author enjoys a Daytona 900 in sunny Somerset – summer 1994

no mention of Triumph at all. It's quiet outside the factory too, no secret prototypes rushing in, no lorry-loads of bikes sweeping out.

But it's a deceptive impression. Inside the factory, there's a sort of subdued freneticism. Everyone is obviously working hard, but no-one is hurrying; the whole place exudes order and control. Bruno Tagliaferri (ex Honda UK) shows us round. He's a very busy man, giving the impression of having half a dozen jobs to do all at once; though given the rate of Triumph's expansion, that's probably true.

Into the stores first. Despite the huge amount of work done in-house, (more than any of the Japanese manufacturers) there are still countless components to be brought in from over 1,000 different suppliers. Instruments, forks, wheels, brakes, electrics are all imported, much of it from Japan. Some people have criticised Triumph for not making a 100% British bike (it's actually 81% by value), which is a little unfair.

Daytonas always had twin piston calipers for the performance image, though eventually most of the range was to follow suit

At the back, the Daytona added a torque arm to the single disc

When Triumph started out, there was no motorcycle assembly industry in Britain and therefore no motorcycle component industry either. A six-person team makes random checks on incoming parts, to check that they are up to scratch.

Not all the parts are ready to use. Con-rods for example (from Japan), crankshafts (Germany), heads and crankcases (Britain) all come as rough-finished forgings and castings. So there's a big machining department, yet it is surprising how many people are needed to run it, thanks to computer-controlled machine tools. Machines outnumber people everywhere – two men look after the machining, one runs the plating plant, but there are 15 CNCs in the turning section alone! It's hardly surprising, given the amount of work needed on engine parts. An example is the crankshaft: first the basic forging is faced and centred, and the oil ways are drilled; then it's stress-relieved in a low temperature oven; journals and pins are

finish ground; the massive gear is cut, and the whole crank deburred and dynamically balanced; it is washed and hardened (plasma nitriding); finally, it's polished, and ready for assembly.

The final assembly track is U-shaped, and you can walk round in a couple of minutes, seeing bare crankcases become engines, have frames attached, then forks, wheels, electrics, bodywork and tank. Every engine has a cold test before being fired up, turned over through the gearbox to test for compression, leaks and vibration. As each bike comes off the end of the line, it gets a sixty point check, plus rolling road test for braking and engine power. It's good to see such close attention being paid to quality, which is also seen in the rejected components at every stage of the process. Better still to hear an aspiring American dealer (Triumph franchise applied for) say that Hinckley was the tidiest bike factory he'd ever seen. Out in the despatch bay, there are France-bound crates bearing words most people thought they'd never see again: "Motorcycle – Fabrique en Angleterre".

Above
Neat detailing behind the seat, with a body colour rather than chrome grabrail

Right
Some described the Daytonas as more sports-touring than sports, but the riding position is still radical enough for anyone with short arms

Smaller, white-faced instruments were always fitted to Daytonas, but otherwise it was all standard Hinckley stuff

In October 1994 Triumph plunged wholeheartedly into retro styling; and arguably, the Triumph heritage meant that they got it right where the Japanese sometimes get it wrong. The new Thunderbird was designed to spearhead a return to the American market – and surprise surprise, there were a few sticky moments regarding the (re-) use of the name! Compression ratio was lowered to 10.0:1, with plenty of low down torque. 36 spoke 2.5-in front and 40-spoke 3.5-in rear rims combined with a 750mm seat height for some of what Willie G Davidosn had so accurately described as "the New Nostalgia." (Photo courtesy Triumph)

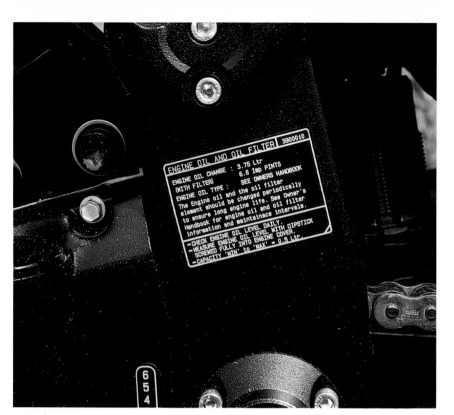

Left
Daytona detailing. The black engine finish was extended to the gearbox and just about everything else mechanical

Below
Daytona Super III – an admission that the standard Daytonas had too much weight and not enough speed. The specification read well, but road testers weren't always impressed

Specifications and Useful Addresses

TRIDENT T150 (1968-75)

Engine:

Type Air cooled pushrod three cylinder
Cylinder head Aluminium alloy, 2 valves
  per cylinder
Cylinder block Aluminium alloy with
  iron liners
Capacity 740cc
Bore × stroke 67mm × 70mm
Compression ratio 9:1 (T150V 9:1)
Carburettors 3 × 27mm Amal Concentrics
Ignition 3 × contact breaker sets and coils
Power 58bhp @ 7,250rpm
Torque 45lb/ft @ 6,900rpm

Transmission:

Primary Drive 3/8 Triplex chain
Clutch Borg & Beck diaphragm type
Gearbox 4-speed (T150V 5-speed)

Cycle Parts:

Frame Brazed tubular steel cradle with
  single downtube (Rocket 3, duplex
  type)
Swinging arm Tubular steel
Wheels
Front Spoked WM2 rim
Rear Spoked WM3 rim
Tyres
Front 3.25 × 19 (T150V, 4.10 × 19)
Rear 4.10 × 19
Suspension
Front Telescopic forks with two-way
  damping and rubber gaiters
Rear Twin dampers, adjustable for
  preload
Brakes
Front 8 inch TLS drum (T150V, 10 inch
  disc)
Rear 7 inch SLS drum

Dimensions:

Length 86.75 in
Width 32.5 in (T150V, 29 in)
Height 44 in
Seat height 32 in
Wheelbase 58 in
Weight (dry) 468lb (T150V, 460lb)

HURRICANE X75 (1973)

Engine:

Type Air-cooled pushrod three cylinder
Cylinder Head Aluminium alloy, 2
  valves per cylinder
Cylinder block Aluminium alloy with
  iron liners
Capacity 740cc
Bore x stroke 67mm x 70mm
Compression ratio 9:1
Carburettors 3 x Amal Concentrics
Ignition 3 x contact breaker sets and
  coils
Power 58bhp @ 7,250rpm
Torque 45lb/ft @ 6,900rpm

Transmission:

Primary drive 3/8 Triplex chain
Clutch Borg & Beck diaphragm type
Gearbox 5-speed

Cycle Parts:

Frame Brazed tubular steel duplex type
Swinging arm Tubular steel
Wheels
Front Spoked, alloy rim
Rear Spoked, alloy rim
Tyres
Front 3.25 x 19
Rear 4.25 x 18
Suspension
Front Telescopic forks, raked and
  extended
Rear Twin dampers, adjustable for
  preload
Brakes
Front 8 inch TLS drum
Rear 7 inch SLS drum

Dimensions:

Seat height 31 in
Wheelbase 60 in
Weight (dry) 444lb

T160 (1975)

Engine:

Type Air cooled pushrod three cylinder
Cylinder head Aluminium alloy, 2 valves
  per cylinder
Cylinder block Aluminium alloy with
  iron liners
Capacity 740cc
Bore x stroke 67mm x 70mm
Compression ratio 9:1
Carburettors 3 x 27mm Amal
  Concentrics Ignition 3 x contact
  breaker sets and coils
Power 58bhp @ 7,250rpm

Transmission:

Primary drive 7/16 duplex chain
Clutch Borg & Beck diaphragm type
Gearbox 5-speed

Cycle Parts:

Frame Brazed tubular steel with single
  downtube
Swinging arm Tubular steel
Wheels
Front Spoked, WM2 rim
Rear Spoked, WM3 rim
Tyres
Front 4.10 x 19
Rear 4.10 x 19
Suspension
Front Telescopic forks, no gaiters
Rear Twin dampers (Girling) with
  preload adjustment
Brakes
Front 10 inch disc
Rear 10 inch disc

Dimensions:

Length 88 in
Width 29 in
Seat height 31 in
Wheelbase 58 in
Weight (dry) 503lb

TRIDENT 750 (1991 on)

Engine:

Type Liquid-cooled DOHC three
  cylinder
Cylinder head Aluminium alloy, 4 valves
  per cylinder
Cylinder block Aluminium alloy, integral
  with crankcase, wet iron liners
Capacity 749cc
Bore x stroke 76 x 55mm
Compression ratio 11:1
Carburettors 3 x Mikuni 36mm flat-slide
  CV
Power 90PS @ 10,000rpm
Torque 50lb/ft @ 8,700rpm

Transmission:

Primary drive Gear
Clutch Wet multiplate
Gearbox 6-speed
Electrics:
Ignition Digital, inductive type
Headlamp 60/55w halogen

Cycle Parts:

Frame High tensile steel spine
Swinging arm Box section aluminium
  alloy with eccentric chain adjuster
Wheels
Front Alloy six spoke (17" x 3)"
Rear Alloy six spoke (18" x 4)"
Tyres
Front 120/70 ZR 17
Rear 160/60 ZR 18
Suspension
Front 43mm hydraulic forks with triple
  rate springs
Rear Monoshock with adjustable preload
Brakes
Front 2 x 296mm discs with 2-piston
  calipers
Rear 1 x 255mm disc with 2-piston
  calliper

Dimensions:

Length 2152mm
Width 760mm
Height 1090mm
Seat height 775mm
Wheelbase 1510mm
Weight (dry) 212kg

TRIDENT 900 (1991 on)

Engine:

Type Liquid cooled DOHC three cylinder
Cylinder head Aluminium alloy, 4 valves per cylinder
Cylinder block Aluminium alloy, integral with crankcase, wet iron liners
Capacity 885cc
Bore x stroke 76 x 65mm
Compression ratio 10.6:1
Carburettors 3 x Mikuni 36mm flat-side CV
Power 100PS @ 9,000rpm
Torque 61lb/ft @ 6,500rpm

Transmission:

Primary drive Gear
Clutch Wet multi-plate
Gearbox 6-speed
Electrics:
Ignition Digital, inductive type
Headlight 60/55w halogen

Cycle Parts:

Frame High tensile steel spine
Swinging arm Box section aluminium alloy with eccentric chain adjuster
Wheels
Front Alloy six spoke (17" x 3)"
Rear Alloy six spoke (18" x 4)"
Suspension
Front 43mm hydraulic forks with triple rate springs
Rear Monoshock with adjustable preload and rebound damping
Brakes
Front 2 x 296mm discs with 2-piston calipers
Rear 1 x 255mm disc with 2-piston calliper

Dimensions:

Length 2152mm
Width 760mm
Height 1090mm
Seat height 775mm
Wheelbase 1510mm
Weight (dry) 212kg

SPRINT 900 (1993 on)

Engine:

Type Liquid-cooled DOHC three cylinder
Cylinder Head Aluminium alloy, 4 valves per cylinder
Cylinder Block Aluminium alloy, integral with crankcase wet iron liners
Capacity 885cc
Bore x stroke 76 x 65mm
Compression ratio 10.6:1
Carburettors 3 x Mikuni 36mm flat-slide CV
Power 98PS @ 9,000rpm
Torque 61lb/ft @ 6,500rpm

Transmission:

Primary drive Gear
Clutch Wet, multiplate
Gearbox 6-speed

Electrics:

Ignition Digital, inductive type
Headlight 2 x 60/55w halogen

Cycle parts:

Frame High tensile steel spine
Swinging arm Box section aluminium alloy with eccentric chain adjuster
Wheels
Front Alloy six spoke (17" x 3")
Rear Alloy six spoke (17" x 4")
Tyres
Front 120/70 ZR 17
Rear 160/60 ZR 18
Suspension
Front 43mm hydraulic forks with dual rate springs
Rear Monoshock with adjustable preload and rebound damping
Brakes
Front 2 x 296mm discs with 2-piston calipers
Rear 1 x 255mm disc with 2-piston calliper

Dimensions:

Length 2152mm
Width 760mm
Height 1265mm
Seat height 775mm
Wheelbase 1490mm
Weight (dry) 215kg

TROPHY 900 (1991 on)

Engine:

Type Liquid-cooled DOHC three cylinder
Cylinder Head Aluminium alloy, 4 valves per cylinder
Cylinder Block Aluminium alloy, integral with crankcase, wet iron liners
Capacity 885cc
Bore x stroke 76 x 65mm
Compression ratio 10.6:1
Carburettors 3 x Mikuni 36mm flat-side CV
Power 98PS @ 9,000rpm
Torque 61lb/ft @ 6,500rpm

Transmission:

Primary drive Gears
Clutch Wet multi-plate
Gearbox 6-speed

Electrics:

Ignition Digital, inductive type
Headlamp 60/55w halogen

Cycle Parts:

Frame High tensile steel spine
Swinging arm Box section aluminium alloy with eccentric chain adjuster
Wheels
Front Alloy three spoke (17" x 3")
Rear Alloy three spoke (17" x 5")
Tyres
Front 120/70 ZR 17
Rear 170/60 ZR 17
Suspension
Front 43mm hydraulic forks with dual rate springs
Rear Monoshock with adjustable preload and rebound damping
Brakes
Front 2 x 310mm floating discs with 4-piston calipers
Rear 1 x 255mm disc with 2-piston calliper

Dimensions:

Length 2152mm
Width 760mm
Height 1270mm
Seat height 780mm
Wheelbase 1490mm
Weight (dry) 217kg

TIGER 900 (1993 on)

Engine:

Type Liquid cooled DOHC three cylinder
Cylinder head Aluminium alloy, 4 valves per cylinder
Cylinder block Aluminium alloy, integral with crankcase, wet iron liners
Capacity 885cc
Bore x stroke 76 x 65mm
Compression ratio 10.6:1
Carburettors 3 x Mikuni 36mm flat-slide CV
Power 85PS @ 8,000rpm
Torque 61lb/ft @ 6,000rpm

Transmission:

Primary Drive Gears
Clutch Wet multiplate
Gearbox 6-speed

Electrics:

Ignition Digital, unductive type
Headlamp 2 x 60/55w halogen

Cycle Parts:

Frame High tensile steel spine
Swinging arm Box section aluminum alloy with eccentric chain adjuster
Wheels
Front 36 spoke alloy rim (19" x 2")
Rear 40 spoke alloy rim (17" x 3")
Tyres
Front 110/80 19 or 100/90 19
Rear 140/80 19
Suspension
Front 43mm hydraulic forks
Rear Monoshock with remote reservoir adjustable for preload, compression and rebound damping
Brakes
Front 2 x 276mm floating discs with 2-piston calipers
Rear 1 x 255mm disc with 2-piston calliper

Dimensions:

Length 2175mm
Width 860mm
Height 1345mm
Seat height 850mm
Wheelbase 1560mm
Weight (dry) 209kg

SPEED TRIPLE (1994 on)

Engine:

Type Liquid-cooled DOHC three cylinder
Cylinder head Aluminium alloy, 4 valves per cylinder
Cylinder block Aluminium alloy, integral with crankcase, wet iron liners
Capacity 885cc
Bore × stroke 76mm × 65mm
Compression ratio 10.6:1
Carburettors 3 × Mikuni 36mm flat-slide CV
Power 98PS @ 9,000rpm
Torque 61lb/ft @ 6,500rpm

Transmission:

Primary Drive Gears
Clutch Wet multiplate
Gearbox 5-speed

Electrics:

Ignition Digital, inductive type
Headlamp 60/55w halogen

Cycle Parts:

Frame High tensile steel spine
Swinging arm Box section aluminum alloy with eccentric chain adjuster
Wheels
Front Alloy three spoke (17" × 3")
Rear Alloy three spoke (17" × 5")
Tyres
Front 120/70 ZR 17
Rear 180/55 ZR 17
Suspension
Front 43mm hydraulic forks with triple rate springs adjustable for compression, rebound damping and spring preload
Rear Monoshock with adjustable preload and rebound damping
Brakes
Front 2 × 310mm floating discs with 4-piston calipers
Rear 1 × 255, disc with 2-piston calliper and frame- mounted torque arm

Dimensions:

Length 2151mm
Width 690mm
Height 1090mm
Seat height 790mm
Wheelbase 1490mm
Weight (dry) 209kg

DAYTONA 900 (1993 on)

Engine:

Type Liquid-cooled DOHC three cylinder
Cylinder head Aluminium alloy, 4 valves per cylinder
Cylinder block Aluminium alloy, integral with crankcase, wet iron liners
Capacity 885cc
Bore × stroke 76mm × 65mm
Compression ratio 10.6:1
Carburettors 3 × Mikuni 36mm flat-slide CV
Power 98PS @ 9,000rpm
Torque 61lb/ft @ 6,500rpm

Transmission:

Primary Drive Gears
Clutch Wet multiplate
Gearbox 6-speed

Electrics:

Ignition Digital, inductive type
Headlamp 2 × 60/55w halogen

Cycle Parts:

Frame High tensile steel spine
Swinging arm Box section aluminum alloy with eccentric chain adjuster
Wheels
Front Alloy three spoke (17" × 3")
Rear Alloy three spoke (17" × 5")
Tyres
Front 120/70 ZR 17
Rear 180/55 ZR 17
Suspension
Front 43mm hydraulic forks with triple rate springs adjustable for compression, rebound damping and spring preload
Rear Monoshock with adjustable preload and rebound damping
Brakes
Front 310mm floating discs with 4-piston calipers
Rear 255mm disc with 2-piston calliper and frame- mounted torque arm

Dimensions:

Length 2152mm
Width 690mm
Height 1185mm
Seat height 790mm
Wheelbase 1490mm
Weight (dry) 213kg

DAYTONA SUPER III (1994 on)

Engine:

Type Liquid-cooled DOHC three cylinder
Cylinder Head Aluminium alloy, 4 valves per cylinder
Cylinder Block Aluminium alloy, integral with crankcase, wet iron liners
Capacity 885cc
Bore × stroke 76mm × 65mm
Compression ratio 12:1
Carburettors 3 × Mikuni 36mm flat-slide CV
Power 113PS @ 9,500rpm
Torque 66lb/ft @ 8,500rpm

Transmission:

Primary Drive Gears
Clutch Wet multiplate
Gearbox 6-speed

Electrics:

Ignition Digital, inductive type
Headlamp 2 × 60/55w halogen

Cycle Parts:

Frame High tensile steel spine
Swinging arm Box section aluminum alloy with eccentric chain adjuster
Wheels
Front Alloy three spoke (17" × 3")
Rear Alloy three spoke (17" × 5")
Tyres
Front 120/70 ZR 17 sport compound
Rear 180/55 ZR 17 sport compound
Suspension
Front 43mm hydraulic forks with triple rate springs adjustable for compression, rebound damping and spring preload
Rear Monoshock with adjustable preload and rebound damping
Brakes
Front 310mm floating discs with 6 piston 'Triumph-6' calipers
Rear 255mm disc with 2-piston calliper and frame- mounted torque arm

Dimensions:

Length 2152mm
Width 690mm
Height 1185mm
Seat height 790mm
Wheelbase 1490mm
Weight (dry) 211kg

USEFUL ADDRESSES

New spares and restoration

L.P. Williams Ltd,
Common Lane,
Kenilworth,
Warks. CV8 2EF

Norman Hyde (dept CMM),
Rigby Close,
Heatcote,
Warwick. CV34 6TL

Restoration and service

Tim Smithells,
Sussex Triples,
12 Walters Cottages,
Wadhurst,
East Sussex.

Pete Gilbert Services,
Units 1 & 2,
Westmans Industrial Estate,
Love Lane,
Burnham-on-Sea,
Somerset. TA8 1EX

Road & Race Preparation

Trident Engineering,
343a Rayners Lane,
Pinner,
Middlesex. HA5 5EN

Clubs

Trident & Rocket 3 Owners Club,
Tim Smithells,
12 Walters Cottages,
Wadhurst,
East Sussex. TN5 6BG

Triumph Owners Club
Mrs M. Mellish, General Secretary,
4 Douglas Avenue,
Harold Wood,
Romford,
Essex. RM3 0UT

*Glory days: Tony Jeffries - another victorious TT partner with Slippery Sam -
with a factory Trident, 1971. Could such glory days return in competition, as
they have done, initially, in the showroom? (Photo courtesy Mick Walker)*